Do You Know
What I Like
About You?

Cynthia Dobbins
9/98

Do You Know What I Like About You?

Jump-Starting Virtues and Values in Your Child

Cynthia Tobias

SERVANT PUBLICATIONS
ANN ARBOR, MICHIGAN

Vine Books is an imprint of Servant Publications especially designed to serve evangelical Christians.

Published in association with the literary agency of Wolgemuth & Hyatt, Inc., 8012 Brooks Chapel Road, Brentwood, Tennessee.

Published by Servant Publications
P.O. Box 8617
Ann Arbor, Michigan 48107

Cover photograph: © S. Chen / Westlight. Used by permission.
Interior photographs: © Skjold Photographs, pages 24, 30, 54, 60, 66, 74, 82, 96, 108, 114
                      © Cynthia Tobias, pages 10, 46, 88
                      © Silvana Clark, pages 16, 38, 102
                      © Shelley Lazarus, E Photography, page 120

98   99   00   10   9   8   7   6   5   4   3   2   1

Printed in the United States of America
ISBN 1-56955-087-5

LIBRARY OF CONGRESS CATALOGING-IN-PUBLICATION DATA

Tobias, Cynthia Ulrich
Do you know what I like about you? : jump-starting virtues and values in your child / Cynthia Tobias.
    p.   cm.
ISBN 1-56955-088-3 (alk. paper)
1. Child rearing–United States.   2. Moral education–United States.   3. Children–United States–Conduct of life.   I.
Title.
HV769.T63   1998
649'.7–dc21   97–44060
                                                                   CIP

Contents

MY
Story

The character of even a child

can be known by the way he acts–

whether what he does

is pure and right.

PROVERBS 20:11, LB

10

It had been one of those very intense parenting days, and by the time I got to bed, I was exhausted. My husband had helped me put our five-year-old twin boys to bed and then had gone into his office to work awhile. As I lay there alone in the darkness trying to go to sleep, I reflected on all the things I had said to the boys during the course of the day: *Don't put the milk back in the refrigerator without the lid on it; Who left the damp towel on the bathroom floor?* and *If you leave these shoes on the floor, the dog will chew them and I won't buy you a new pair!*

Nothing bad, of course, just the run-of-the-mill mom stuff—but I felt guilty. I wanted my children to remember loving statements coming from me, not just custodial comments. I made a decision right then and there to start a new tradition the very next morning.

Michael, our very strong-willed twin, was the first little boy to peek his head around the corner of our bedroom, very early in the morning. He stood for a moment in the doorway, surveying the best place to land, and then came charging into bed between Daddy and me.

I put my arm around him and whispered, "Hey, Mike, do you know what I like about you?" He snuggled in. "What?" I held him close and thought back over the past two or three days.

"Well, I love how you opened the door for your teacher without being asked, and I especially like the way you shared that new toy with your brother even though you didn't have to, and you know what else?"

Mike just basked in the praise and encouragement as I pointed out several more positive things he had done recently. Then it was Robert's turn. Another energetic twin wiggled into bed, and I started all over:

"Hey, Rob, do you know what I like about you?"

When my husband, John, and I talked later about the new tradition, he agreed it was a good idea. I explained: "I know I can consider myself a better parent if anyone at any time stops either of the boys, kneels down to their eye level, and asks, 'What does your mom like best about you?' and they can remember specific things. After all, our children know we love them, but do they really know why?"

I hope this book will help you focus on dozens of ways you can work to affirm your children's positive behavior. I hope after you read it you will be able to tell them *specifically* what you love about them. By focusing on their positive traits, you will enrich not only their lives but the life of your family as well. (You may be amazed to find out how much focusing on the positive will improve relationships between all of your family's members.) Affirmation can help you spark the values and virtues that form moral character and integrity in each child.

After less than six months of repeating our morning tradition every few days, Michael showed up at my bedside one morning. Instead of jumping into bed right away, he stood beside me and whispered:

"Mommy?"

"Yes, Mike?"

"Do you know what I like about you?"

I rolled over and my eyes popped wide open. Wow! What a great kid!

all My Tomorrows

All my tomorrows

Depend on your love,

For I am small

And very vulnerable.

I see

Only through your eyes

And feel

Only through your touch.

My life is a mirror,

And your reflection forms my image.

My heart knows only the boundaries

You set for me,

And my mind expands only

As you let me learn.

My love for you is formed on trust,

And can never be destroyed

Except by your power.

CYNTHIA ULRICH TOBIAS

JUMP-STARTING
Your Child's Courage to Stand Up for Convictions

⌇

Whatever happens, conduct yourselves in a manner worthy of the gospel of Christ. Then, whether I come and see you or only hear about you in my absence, I will know that you stand firm in one spirit, contending as one man for the faith of the gospel without being frightened in any way by those who oppose you.

PHILIPPIANS 1:27–28a, NIV

Kelli, a quiet, conscientious fourteen-year-old, attended a public high school in the middle of a very liberal city. Her greatest struggle in ninth grade was not academic but spiritual. When she learned about a "Meet Me at the Flagpole" event for teens to honor the National Day of Prayer, it was something she felt she should do. Although several other kids in her church youth group had expressed interest in participating, most of her classmates had never even heard of the event. When she mentioned it to them, their reaction was swift and abrupt: "What a dumb idea!" they told her. "If you show up at the flagpole and pray, everybody in school will think you're strange. You'll get stuck with everybody calling you 'weird' for the rest of your life. Just pray by yourself at home!"

The night before the "Meet Me at the Flagpole" event, Kelli's dad could sense she was really struggling. "Kelli, is everything OK?" She looked up at him and made a valiant effort to hold back her tears.

"Dad, I really want to do the right thing. I feel that praying at the flagpole is something I should do tomorrow, but I don't know one other person who will be there. What if I get there and no one else shows up? What if my friends find out and think I'm just weird?"

Kelli's dad reached out and put his arm around her shoulders. "Kelli, I have always been so proud of you and your stand for Christ. This may be one of the hardest tests you've had so far, and I know you'll make the right decision. I'll take you to school tomorrow, and whatever you decide to do about the flagpole prayer is all right with me."

It was barely dawn when Kelli woke her dad. "Dad?" she whispered, "will you take me to school now? I'm going to pray at the flagpole—even if I'm the only one there."

Her father's heart ached as he watched his precious girl grip the car's armrest all the way to school. Her face was pale but determined as she smiled at him. "It's OK, Dad. I prayed about this, and all night long I kept hearing the same song in my head: 'Though none go with me, I'll follow Jesus; no turning back, no turning back.' I guess being considered weird wouldn't be the worst thing that could happen to me."

As the car rounded the corner in front of the school, Kelli noticed quite a crowd had gathered—but not to pray. She recognized many of her friends and lots of other kids who were considered "popular" huddled near the flagpole. They were giggling and pointing at two students standing near the flagpole with their heads bowed in prayer. Momentary panic flashed across Kelli's face as she opened the car door.

Her dad reached over and took her hand. "Kelli, just remember, I love you no matter which of those two groups out there you join." Kelli smiled and nodded as she left the safety of the car and headed across the street. Her dad felt tears stinging his eyes as he watched his daughter bravely walk over toward the flagpole. How he wished he could go along, holding her hand for support. For a long, torturous minute, he watched her join the two students at the flagpole and bow her head in front of some of the most influential kids in the school. He was so proud that she had the courage to stand up for her convictions.

Suddenly, several teens broke loose from the watching crowd. Together they moved over to the flagpole and stood by Kelli. She lifted her head long enough to smile at them before continuing her prayer. As her dad watched, the numbers of students in the two groups began to shift. Before he finally drove away, the largest group by far was made up of those bowing their heads at the flagpole. He eagerly looked forward to talking with Kelli. He already knew exactly what he was going to say: "Kelli, I think you made the difference. I think those kids were waiting for *you*."

We Will Find Our Way

My candle is but a flicker

And I have no other light.

You are my friend—

Help me now.

Please, reach over

And light your fire

Against the dark.

It may be small,

But it will encourage

My tiny flicker,

And together

We will find our way.

Cynthia Ulrich Tobias

COURAGE OF CONVICTIONS

As early as possible, we need to teach our children the value of having the courage to stand up for right and wrong, to hold to their convictions even when those convictions are unpopular, to express their faith in God. Affirming our children's courage when it comes to standing up for their beliefs will help create for all of us a world with stronger moral values.

GIVE IT A TRY

1. When was the last time you saw or heard your child stand up for a belief? Even if it's for something as seemingly insignificant as not cheating on a test or not watching a questionable TV program, let your child know how much you value the decision.
2. Talk to your children about ways they can encourage others when they see them standing up for what they believe.
3. Pointing out to your child specific news stories or articles about people who have stood up for their beliefs can be a powerful example that there are still some people who are not afraid to stand up and speak out for their convictions.

JUMP-STARTING
Your Child's Love for Learning God's Word

&

How can a young man keep his way pure?

By living according to your word.

I seek you with all my heart;

do not let me stray from your commands.

I have hidden your word in my heart

that I might not sin against you.

PSALM 119:9–11, NIV

"**M**ommy, do you know what my favorite Bible verse is?" Six-year-old Brandon clutched a large, already-worn children's Bible in his hands. His mom, Cheryl, stopped clearing the table and knelt down by her son.

"Brandon, you know so many verses, I just don't know which one would be your favorite," she admitted. Brandon paused and frowned in concentration.

"Actually," he said thoughtfully, "I think I have *two* favorite verses." Cheryl smiled and chuckled softly to herself. Brandon sounded so grown-up when he talked about the Bible. He continued, "I like Psalm 23–'The Lord is my shepherd'–and I like John 3:16–'For God so loved the world.'" Cheryl bent to give him a hug.

"Brandon, I am so proud of you for knowing so much of God's Word already. You know, there are a lot of grown-ups who don't know as much about the Bible as you do at six. You have memorized a new verse every month for two years now, and I know God is very pleased with you."

Brandon grinned at his mother. "I want to read my Bible every day," he vowed.

"And I want to keep learning new verses 'til I know all about God."

Cheryl nodded and turned back to her work at the kitchen table. Brandon tugged at her skirt. "Mommy, aren't you going to help me learn a new verse now?" he asked. She quickly surveyed the messy kitchen and thought of how little time there was to get everything straightened before bedtime. Then she looked at her son's face, as he eagerly held the Bible up toward her.

"Brandon, do you know what I like about you?" she asked. "I like how you keep me interested in the Bible, too. We should never get too busy to read and memorize God's Word. Let's see which verse we should learn next."

Brandon put the Bible on the table and hopped up into his mother's lap. She took a deep breath and opened the pages of her son's favorite Book. She offered a silent prayer as she held her son close: *Lord, keep me as eager for your Word as this young child is.*

"Mommy?" Brandon said. "Let's memorize *your* favorite verse."

Cheryl nodded. "Brandon, that's a great idea. Run get my Bible."

First Place

"In quietness and confidence,"

The Lord reminded me,

"Is where you'll find that needed strength

To have and do and be."

"The thousand things that you must do

Must all begin with one—

And that's a quiet time of prayer

And speaking through God's Son."

"Thank you, Lord," I sighed through tears,

"I know without a doubt

That all of my frustrations

Are because I left you out."

Then silently I knelt and prayed

And found a quiet peace;

Strength returned, my smile came back,

And all my worries ceased.

CYNTHIA ULRICH TOBIAS

LEARNING TO LOVE GOD'S WORD

There is no better use of your child's time than reading and memorizing God's Word. It is God's Word that brings salvation, instruction for right living, the courage to live for God, an understanding and a view of God that is faith building, and the promise of eternal life. It is the foundation stone in building a Christian life in your child. You will be amazed at how early young children can begin to memorize Bible verses and how well they understand Scripture meanings once they are explained. Work at setting a good example yourself by reading and memorizing the Word, and everyone will grow!

GIVE IT A TRY

1. Set aside a time each day in your family schedule for reading the Bible and working on Scripture memorization. Even if you miss some days, make the habit important. Let your children help you decide what the best time would be and which verses they would like to learn.

2. If your children are motivated by watching television, try showing some of the excellent biblical videos available at your local Christian bookstores. Nest Entertainment (1-800-447-5958) also has an outstanding series of Old and New Testament animated videos that help children focus on Scripture and Bible stories while they enjoy the newest applications of media technologies.

JUMP-STARTING
Your Child's Willingness to Serve Others

∾

If you must choose, take a good name rather
than great riches; for to be held in loving
esteem is better than silver and gold.

PROVERBS 22:1, LB

"I'll get it!" Tina raced off the field to capture the runaway ball. Her dad, Jim, cheered proudly from the sidelines. The man sitting next to him turned to him sympathetically.

"I guess you feel kinda sorry for your daughter since she can't really participate in the game," he said.

Jim shook his head while he cheered and gave his daughter the "thumbs up" sign as she brought the ball back.

"Oh, no," he replied as the game continued. "That precious little girl sitting on the bench over there is the hardest worker on that team. They wouldn't know what to do without her."

The man looked a little puzzled. "Is she the manager or something?"

Jim grinned. "Well, she certainly does her share of letting the other players know what to do, but she doesn't really have an official title. In fact, I think she likes to call herself 'helper'—that's the only position she wants to play."

Suddenly Tina appeared in front of her dad breathlessly.

"Dad! There's a time out and I need to find a Band-Aid for Sarah!"

Jim scrambled to his feet. "Good job, Tina. I'm glad you noticed what Sarah needed. That's why this team needs *you*! Let's go get that Band-Aid from the car, Sport."

It wasn't until Jim and Tina walked away that the man noticed the limp in Tina's step and the left arm that didn't move naturally at her side. When Jim returned, the man spoke again.

"So I guess the only thing your daughter is able to do is be the 'gofer,' huh?"

Jim turned and looked at him. "Actually, Tina can do anything she really puts her mind to," he replied. "Her physical limitations don't really determine what makes her happy. From the time she was a toddler, she just always wanted to do things for people. She truly has a servant's heart."

The man looked skeptical. "That's my daughter over there," he said, pointing to the pitcher's mound. "She can do anything she wants to, also. But she's a leader–she'll never be anybody's servant."

Jim didn't hesitate in his reply. "Every child has natural gifts. Tina's is the gift of helping," he explained. "We've pointed out to her how important it is to recognize and meet the needs of others. We've told her how proud we are when she plays even the smallest part in a victory or success. Every piece of the puzzle is necessary."

The other man snorted. "Now, that sounds like you're just making her feel good about losing. I want my daughter to win—not just look for excuses for why she *didn't*." The game was almost over. Jim struggled for a way to make this man understand what a fine person Tina was and how content she was to serve others. Suddenly the shout of victory sounded, and Tina's teammates were screaming with success. Amidst hats being flung in the air, together they hoisted one of the girls onto their shoulders and took a victory lap around the field.

The man sitting beside Jim squinted into the sunshine before he recognized the girl being carried by the team. He turned to Jim. "Why are they carrying *your* daughter?" he asked. "She didn't even play in the game."

Jim smiled and applauded as the team passed by. "I think maybe the girls know how to celebrate the real winners," he replied proudly.

↩

The Best of Who I Am

I know that I can't run and jump

And play the way you do;

I know my mind sometimes won't take

The same pathways as you.

I know you wonder if I'm sad

Because I'm not the same,

Or if sometimes I feel real mad

Since I can't join in the game.

You need to know—I don't ask why;

I believe that God knows best,

And he has in me his own design,

And on this truth I rest:

It's not what I can't do;

Instead it's what I can—

I can sure love you,

Just the way God planned.

His design shows in me

His eternal tapestry—

To be the best that I can be

With who I am.

CYNTHIA ULRICH TOBIAS

A WILLINGNESS TO SERVE OTHERS

The Bible tells us that "the last shall be first and the first shall be last," and yet we often don't teach our children the importance of serving others. A true servant's heart is a rare commodity in these days of cutthroat competition and scrambling to the top of the corporate ladder. Although we must help equip our children to survive and succeed, we dare not overlook the significance of learning to recognize and meet the needs of others.

GIVE IT A TRY

1. Make a game of helping your child find ways to serve someone in his or her life every day. For example, keep a chart and paste on stickers or give points each day for good deeds done for others. Encourage anonymity; point out the importance of doing good just for the sake of helping, not for being given any credit.
2. Help your children discover the "servants" in their lives: who are the ones who help *them* most? How can they recognize and appreciate them?

JUMP-STARTING
Your Child's Sense of Humor

❧

A relaxed attitude lengthens a man's life.

PROVERBS 14:30, LB

"**K**nock, knock." Although Debbie wasn't really in the mood to hear a five-year-old's idea of a joke, she decided to humor her son. Robert dearly loved to tell jokes.

"Who's there?" she asked.

"Arthur."

"Arthur who?" She braced herself for his response.

"Arthur the baby!" He was laughing so hard he doubled over.

"Robert." she explained for the hundredth time, "that isn't funny! You need a punch line!" He shrugged and grinned.

"OK," he agreed. "Knock, knock."

She was suspicious, but took the bait anyway.

"Who's there?"

"Arthur."

"Arthur who?"

"Arthur the baby! Ha! Ha! Ha!" He was so tickled that Debbie laughed in spite of herself. His eyes were sparkling, and he was holding his stomach as he laughed and laughed. Debbie wondered how long had it been since *she* had experienced such pure, unadulterated delight.

"Robert, do you know what a joke is?"

His eyes were twinkling up at her. His small head nodded vigorously. "Oh, yes, Mommy. A joke is what makes other people laugh when they need to."

Debbie smiled lovingly. No one ever made her laugh as much as Robert. Sometimes she would burst into giggles just watching him with his friends.

"Robert," she said more seriously, "you have a gift, you know. It's a gift you give other people by letting them laugh and enjoy themselves. It's one of the things I like most about you."

Robert's face broke into a wide grin. "I like making people laugh," he admitted. "But sometimes people get tired of my jokes."

Debbie put her arm around him. "Well, as you get older," she replied, "you will be able to figure out what makes people laugh and what doesn't. For right now, it's just great that you want those around you to be happy."

Robert looked pleased. "So, Mommy, why don't *you* tell *me* a joke?" he asked.

Debbie paused. Suddenly she hated to admit to her son how little she laughed these days. "Robert," she said slowly, "I can't even think of one right now. I just might have to go to the library and check out a few joke books."

Robert looked excited. "Oh, boy! That would be great!" He paused. "I know a good joke right now, though," he said.

Debbie answered without even thinking.

"What?"

"Knock, knock."

She groaned. "Oh, no!"

Robert was already laughing.

Let's Have Some Fun

They say most cats should have a tail,

And dogs should have some hair,

You really shouldn't tickle folks

And never take a dare.

You can't just always hug someone

Or hold a person's hand,

And you must play an instrument

If you would join the band.

But let's not think the way they do,

Let's stir things up a bit!

Let's have some fun, enjoy ourselves—

Let's stand instead of sit!

Let's find a cat that has no tail,

A dog that has no hair;

Let's tickle someone just for fun,

And take a double dare.

Let's make a face and laugh out loud

Then grab a grown-up's hand,

Let's give someone a great big hug

Then pretend you're in the band.

CYNTHIA ULRICH TOBIAS

A SENSE OF HUMOR

A sense of humor is a wonderful gift, both to the person who has it and to those with whom it is shared. Teaching your children to recognize and cultivate a sense of humor can help them keep life in perspective and maintain a positive attitude amidst even the worst conditions.

GIVE IT A TRY

1. Have a joke-telling night in your family. Set some guidelines—such as no making fun of other people's sense of humor. To make sure no one feels bad if others don't get the punch line, try having a code word for laughter. For example, when the punch line is given and no one laughs, if you say the word "radio," everyone agrees to laugh uproariously, whether they get it or not.

2. Make it a practice to share humorous stories with your children. Keep a file of anecdotes, stories, and illustrations from newspapers, magazines, and books. Have the file ready at a moment's notice for a rainy day, a crabby afternoon, or some quiet family time. Periodically, take a vote on the top ten favorites.

JUMP-STARTING
Your Child's Kindness to Others

We stand true to the Lord whether others honor us or despise us, whether they criticize us or commend us. We are honest, but they call us liars.

2 CORINTHIANS 6:8, LB

"This will be the best birthday party ever!" Richard's eyes were dancing. His mom was trying to make out the invitations, but she was having trouble getting her soon-to-be-eight-year-old son to concentrate on writing down his guest list.

"Richard," she said patiently, "we need to get these invitations out today. Whom do you want to invite?" Richard paused thoughtfully. "Well, I know who I *don't* want to invite," he replied. His mom looked surprised. Richard was one of the most sociable and friendly kids she'd ever met. It was hard to imagine that he had an enemy.

"Richard, why would you say that?" she asked.

He furrowed his brow and shrugged. "I don't know. I just don't want Thomas to wreck my party–that's all. He's so mean to me at school. I don't want him to come to our house."

His mom pulled him close for a moment and looked into his face. "Richard, I'm sorry if Thomas has made your life miserable at school. Of course you don't have to invite anyone you don't *want* to have at your party, but do you think Thomas will wonder why he was the only one in your class who didn't receive an invitation?"

Richard frowned. "Hmmm, maybe."

His mom watched the struggle on his face. "Richard, you've made friends with some of the meanest, shyest, and most obnoxious kids at your school. You have a natural ability to reach out to others and make them feel good. What happened with Thomas?" Richard shook his head and sighed. "I don't know. Let's send him an invitation. I'll see if I can try to be his friend."

The day of the party was gray and overcast, and a light rain had begun to fall. The family room was packed with children celebrating Richard's birthday, but the guest of honor was nowhere to be found. Richard's dad found his wife in the kitchen.

"Where in the world is Richard?" he asked. "The party is going full blast without him."

She nodded toward the kitchen window, which looked out into the front yard. Coming up the walkway were Richard and Thomas. Richard had his arm thrown around Thomas' shoulder.

"Our thoughtful son went out there to personally greet his most difficult guest," she replied. Just then the door opened and the two boys came in.

"Son, I'm proud of you," his dad said as he patted Richard on the shoulder.

"Me, too," his mom added.

"I know," Richard answered with a little grin. "Come on, Thomas, the party's in here."

As the boys disappeared around the corner, Richard's mom overheard Thomas say, "I still think you're a geek, Richard," to which Richard laughingly replied, "Yeah, well, it's OK if you want to think that. I get the gifts anyway. Maybe you should try being a geek, too."

⇆

Love in Earthen Vessels

We have love

Contained in an earthen vessel,

And we pour it out

With as much care

And in the greatest abundance

We can,

Even though we can't always tell

how it is received

Or the good it has done.

And God,

In his infinite love and understanding,

Keeps our earthen pitcher full,

Directs the flow of love,

And pours the contents

Directly from his own pitcher

Onto the places

We may have missed.

Cynthia Ulrich Tobias

KINDNESS

Recently someone wrote a book about random acts of kindness. That's a great idea, but an even better one is plotting to be kind. Kindness and compassion for others can be your child's greatest assets when it comes to making the world a better place to live. We need to raise a generation of thoughtful, tender, kind people. We can do that with the children we are raising now. Teaching our children to think of the welfare of others, even when it's inconvenient, can help them cultivate a lifetime of friendships and positive relationships.

GIVE IT A TRY

1. Encourage your children to help you keep an eye out for news stories or accounts of people doing acts of kindness for others. Point out how each child can do the same kind of good deeds every day. Put your stories in a scrapbook so that you can go back to them from time to time.

2. Find some books to read with your children that tell stories about bullies or others who act mean and unkind. Help them figure out what the possible endings could be before you read the one in the book. Emphasize that bullies never really win.

JUMP-STARTING
Your Child's Love for Learning

∽

A wise teacher makes learning a joy.

PROVERBS 15:2, LB

> ## All About Me
>
> *My name is Allison Baker.*
> *I love to ask questions and to draw.*
> *I don't like to be questioned by anybody.*
>
> Signed, Allison Baker, Age 9

The assignment was brief, the response so characteristic of Allison. Sandra smiled and tucked the piece of notebook paper back into Allie's backpack. Allison was her third and last child, an unexpected bundle who entered the world with great strength and determination.

"Where's my homework?" Allison rounded the corner and plunked herself down at the kitchen table. Her mom pointed to the backpack and Allison nodded.

"Allie, I just want to tell you how much I love your 'All About Me' assignment. I think you really captured the heart of who you are." Allison frowned suspiciously.

"What do you mean?" she asked.

"I've never met anyone who is as thorough and careful about getting the facts and finding the right answers as you are. It's a wonderful quality, and I'm so proud of your desire to learn about so many things. Someday you will probably discover some wonderful new scientific theory, medicine, or invention to change the world and make our lives better."

Allison shrugged and tried to pretend indifference. Her mom gave her a quick hug.

"One thing is for sure, Sweetheart. You are definitely going to leave a significant impression on the world just because you were here. I hope you keep your determination to learn for the rest of your life."

Allison nodded. "Mom, why do you think it's so important to learn? And how do you know why you've actually learned something, anyway? And how come ..."

Sandra grinned and rolled her eyes. "OK, OK! I'm going to have a tough time keeping up with you! What was the first question again?"

Black and White

You are the kind

That must have it

In black and white—

No hazy gray mists,

Vague romantic notions,

Or double-meaning phrases.

You want to take it

As it comes—

No philosophizing,

Compromising,

Or idealizing,

But there must be

People like you

To hold deeper thinkers

Close enough to the surface

To keep them from drowning.

CYNTHIA ULRICH TOBIAS

LOVE OF LEARNING

Encouraging your children to learn could be one of the very best gifts you will ever give them. Information changes more rapidly than anyone can anticipate, but those who know how to keep learning will never be far behind.

If your child knows how to learn, the options and choices will belong to them, and they will not be at the mercy of others.

GIVE IT A TRY

1. Make it a habit to ask your children frequently what they would like to learn more about–what really captures their interest. Encourage them to visit science centers, aquariums, and special events in your area that can foster learning and new discoveries. Keep a short journal with notes about what seems to interest each child most, and look for ways to keep their interests alive.

2. Try making a game of "What I Know That You Probably Don't." Challenge your children to come home with facts and knowledge you may not have–and compare "notes." You can often help your child appreciate new knowledge just by reinforcing the fact that he or she may actually be smarter than you in many ways!

JUMP-STARTING
Your Child's Spirit of Optimism

The backslider gets bored with himself;

the godly man's life is exciting.

PROVERBS 14:14, LB

I t had been a bad day for Jack. As he tried to open the gate, he fumbled with the latch he should have replaced weeks ago. Then he stubbed his toe on the uneven flagstones that really needed to be reset. The last straw was when he put his foot on the porch step and heard it splinter. *Oh, brother!* he thought. *The whole place is falling down, and I'm not due for any extra overtime money this month.* He was mumbling under his breath when Tracy, his ten-year-old daughter, appeared at the front door. "Daddy!" she called happily. "I'm so glad you're home!"

Jack smiled in spite of himself. Tracy was always such a ray of sunshine. "Hi, Honey, how was your day at school?"

"Oh, Daddy, it was so great! I just love Mrs. Connor, and she told me I was one of the nicest students she'd ever had in her class!"

Jack put his arm around Tracy. "Now, that's the truth," he said. "Tracy, you have the gift of 'sparkle.'" His daughter looked puzzled, and he explained, "Trace, some people just naturally light up the room when they're in it. They sparkle, their eyes twinkle, and everyone feels happier just being around them. You are that kind of person, Sweetheart, and I love coming home because you're here. You always have something positive and uplifting to say to me."

Tracy's face was beaming. "Thanks, Daddy! It's *easy* to be happy around *you!*" Jack grinned. "See? I'm a terrible crab, and you love me anyway. You are a real treasure!"

Tracy was already running to the front door. "Quick, Daddy, I hear Mom coming. Let's make her happy to come home, too. Do you think she's had a bad day?"

Jack watched his daughter proudly. "It doesn't matter, Tracy. I guarantee her day will always improve when she comes home to you! Please, always keep your positive attitude. The world sure needs people like you."

"Thanks, Daddy. I'm going to go show Mom my sparkle!"

Surprised by Life

Excitement, like beauty,

Must lie in the eye of the beholder.

Anticipate surprises—

Let life be exciting—

Expect to find new discoveries

Even when looking in old,

   worn-out places.

The heart has a large capacity

For excitement,

A keen desire for surprises.

Unfortunately, the heart's eye

Too often overlooks

The truly beautiful and exciting,

And underscores the ordinary.

Let life surprise you—

It rarely disappoints an

   expectant seeker.

CYNTHIA ULRICH TOBIAS

YOUR CHILD'S OPTIMISM

Those who possess and use optimism will always be a valuable part of our society. The ability to impart hope and encouragement can hold the world together while others try to tear it apart.

If you have a child who is naturally gifted with optimism, do everything you can to keep that positive spirit intact. While we should not build unrealistic expectations, we can underscore the importance of a trust and faith in the Creator who is still in control of his creation.

GIVE IT A TRY

1. Do your best to notice the times when your child is being positive and optimistic. Talk about what constitutes a positive attitude and how being upbeat and cheerful can encourage others to do the same.
2. Strike a deal with all family members. Every time anyone says something negative about something or someone, he or she must say three positive things, too. You'll be surprised how quickly the negative comments will be minimized.

JUMP-STARTING
Your Child's Patriotism

⤸

You then, my son, be strong in the grace that is in
Christ Jesus. And the things you have heard me
say in the presence of many witnesses entrust to
reliable men who will also be qualified to
teach others. Endure hardship with us
like a good soldier of Christ Jesus.

2 TIMOTHY 2:1-3, NIV

The game was about to start. Eight-year-old Ryan was excited to be attending with a very important person–his grandpa. The announcer's voice boomed out over the loudspeaker: "Ladies and gentlemen, please stand for the singing of our national anthem." Ryan stood beside his grandpa and put his right hand over his heart, just like Grandpa did.

Grandpa looked down at the young boy standing beside him and smiled. Ryan was already learning the importance of good citizenship, and Grandpa made a mental note to tell Ryan how proud his actions made him feel.

Ryan, in the meantime, was wondering what the national anthem really meant. He looked around and noticed there weren't many people singing the words. Ryan glanced up at his grandpa and was surprised to see tears rolling down his face. Ryan frowned with concern. Grandpa didn't seem to be sick or hurt–why was he crying? The song ended, and the crowd erupted into thunderous applause as the ballplayers took the field.

"Grandpa!" Ryan shouted above the noise. "Why are you crying?"

Grandpa turned and smiled. "I'll tell you later!" he replied.

When Ryan and Grandpa were riding home, Ryan brought up the subject again. "Grandpa, are you OK? I saw you crying before the game."

"Ryan," Grandpa said soberly, "I almost always cry when they bring out our flag and sing our national anthem.""

Ryan looked puzzled. "Why?" he asked. Grandpa pulled the car into a restaurant parking lot and turned toward Ryan.

"Well, you see, I spent several years in the armed forces. I fought in two major wars, and I know how important our freedom is to us. So many of my friends lost their lives in the wars, and I came close to dying more than once. But every one of us was prepared to die in order to keep our country free. Whenever I see our flag or sing our national anthem, I remember how precious are the lives that have been given in the service of our country. I'd be proud to do it all over again."

Ryan looked thoughtful. "But the wars were a long time ago, Grandpa. We don't have to fight anymore." Before Grandpa could reply, Ryan quickly added, "But if we *did* have wars, I would want to fight for our country, too."

Grandpa shook his head. "Ryan, war is a terrible thing, and I hope you never have to actually go to war. But I'm very proud to see you showing respect for our flag and to hear you say you'd stand up for our freedom."

Ryan was silent for a moment before he spoke again. Grandpa had pulled back out into traffic to finish the trip home.

"Grandpa?"

"Yes, Ryan?"

"Do you think you could teach me all the words to our national anthem? I think I need to sing the whole song next time."

"Ryan, I would consider it an honor to do that for such a grand young citizen," Grandpa replied.

God, Bless America

In a day when complaints are so easily made,

When the rumors of wars serve to make us afraid,

When inflation would smother, and money lose power—

God, bless America in our lowest hour.

When evil still creeps into what was once good;

When good honest people don't do what they should,

As morals decay and bring great despair—

God, help America to remember you care.

We fought for our freedom and died for our rights,

But it won't mean a thing unless God is our might.

Lord, lead us again to your almighty throne;

Remind our great country we're not on our own.

Oh, Lord, we can't lose it—it was too dearly bought.

So, God, bless America—it's the best thing we've got!

CYNTHIA ULRICH TOBIAS

THE IMPORTANCE OF PATRIOTISM

Many children do not realize the importance of their heritage of freedom and independence. A sense of patriotism can begin with something as small as an explanation of the meaning of our flag or national anthem. Our children need to appreciate what keeps their country free.

GIVE IT A TRY

1. When was the last time any of your children made a comment or asked a question about our country or national heritage? Take the next opportunity to talk with them about their interest, and help them better understand patriotism.

2. Together as a family, watch some videos about historical figures who stood for truth and liberty. Discuss the positive attributes of the characters and point out similar ones in your children.

JUMP-STARTING
Your Child's Ability to Be a Peacemaker

⬤

Happy are those who strive for peace–they
shall be called the sons of God.

MATTHEW 5:9, LB

"You give that back, and I mean it!"

"NO! You change that channel for me right now or I'll never give it back!"

"Change it yourself!"

"MOM!"

Marcy could hear two of her children fighting from where she stood, all the way out in the kitchen. She felt herself getting ready to scream at them when her youngest son rounded the corner.

"Let me talk to them, Mom," David said pleasantly. Before she could protest, he went into the living room where his siblings were still threatening to tear each other apart.

"Larry, if you give back Sally's toy, I think she'll let you change the channel. You will, won't you, Sally?"

Marcy watched in amazement as her two feuding children stopped in their tracks and considered their brother's suggestion.

Sally frowned. "Well, I think he should tell me he's sorry for taking it in the first place," she replied.

As Larry was taking a deep breath to yell that he would never apologize, David interrupted him. "Wait, Larry. I don't think you wanted to make Sally cry. You aren't a mean person."

Larry shrugged. "Nah, I don't like to see girls cry. Here's your stupid toy back," he mumbled, casually tossing the doll back to his sister.

David nodded his head. "Thanks, Larry. Sally, will you be nicer to Larry now?"

She shrugged and nodded. "Yeah, I could do that for a while."

David moved over to the TV and changed the channel to Larry's favorite program. "Larry, do you think Sally could watch one of her favorite programs as soon as you're finished with this one? Maybe even a video? What do you think?"

"Yeah, sure. Whatever."

As David walked back into the kitchen, his brother and sister were sitting quietly in front of the screen. Marcy grabbed her son and gave him a hug.

"David, I declare, you have better ways of solving arguments and bringing peace than most *adults* I know!" David seemed embarrassed and looked out the window.

Marcy gently turned his head toward her and looked directly into his eyes.

"Being a peacemaker and helping people solve problems without harsh words or fighting is a gift–a wonderful gift! You're going to do great things with your life, mostly because people are going to really need your ability to help them compromise and live harmoniously with each other."

David smiled and looked pleased. "I don't think it's that big a deal," he said. But the look on his face told his mom her words of praise had made him feel pretty special.

"Can you be a peacemaker for a living?" he asked. Marcy grinned.

"David, if anyone can negotiate a good salary, *you* can!"

Do What You Can

The course of love,

The poets say,

Is never very smooth;

For harsh and cutting words are said

Along with those that soothe.

A smile today could be a frown

With any passing mood,

And what was meant to be polite

Could turn out very rude.

You must be gentle, and believe

That all will turn out best.

Do what you can

   with what you have,

And trust God for the rest.

CYNTHIA ULRICH TOBIAS

BLESSED ARE THE PEACEMAKERS

Peacemaking is a wonderful and rare virtue. If you have a child who naturally helps others compromise and get along, encourage this gift. Peacemakers are the ambassadors, the counselors, the pastors of our world. They are often the negotiators who are vital in bringing enemies and opposing viewpoints into agreement so diverse people can live together in harmony.

GIVE IT A TRY

1. Watch for opportunities to point out how someone in the news is helping to bring peace to the world or to local situations. Point out how your own peacemaker child is doing similar things on a smaller scale.

2. Play the "what if" game with your child. What if you saw two children fighting over a ball on the playground at school? What would be the appropriate action? What if you were president of the United States and you saw two countries fighting? What would you do?

3. Encourage and praise your child's desire to bring peace to every situation, but point out that it is not always in his or her power to solve the problem. Affirm the fact that even playing a small part in the process can make a difference.

JUMP-STARTING
Your Child's Thoughtfulness

In everything, do to others what you
would have them do to you, for
this sums up the Law and the Prophets.

MATTHEW 7:12, NIV

"Mommy, we need to get some Trix cereal." Four-year-old Rachel wore a very serious expression as she pulled her mother down to her level in the supermarket aisle. Karen looked surprised as she knelt beside her daughter.

"Rachel, you don't even *like* cereals that have all the colors. Why do you want Trix?"

"Mommy, we have to keep it in our kitchen," Rachel insisted. "'Cause on TV those kids will never give the rabbit any Trix, and I think that's really mean. If I ever see that rabbit, I want to make sure I have some Trix to give him."

Karen had to think for a moment, so Rachel quickly reminded her of the commercial.

"Remember, Mommy? The rabbit loves Trix and always tries to get some, and those kids take them away before he can eat any. They say, 'Sorry, Rabbit, Trix are for kids.' I want to make sure we keep some cereal for him in case he comes to our house to look."

Karen smiled at her daughter's sincere face, and put her arm around her small shoulders.

"Oh, Rachel, that is so thoughtful! You have a very kind heart, and I am so proud of how you are always thinking of others. You are a very special little girl, and I would be pleased to buy that box of cereal for your rabbit."

Rachel grinned and hugged her mom. "Mommy, he's not *my* rabbit," she protested. "He's nobody's rabbit, but you shouldn't be mean to him."

Karen stood up and took Rachel's hand. "You're absolutely right," she agreed. "Let's make sure we put that cereal on a shelf he can reach if he shows up in our kitchen."

As the pair walked happily down the aisle, Rachel sneaked a peek behind her and whispered, "Come see me, Rabbit, and I'll be your friend!"

Thoughtfulness

Look for the good in each person,

Find something nice to say—

Smile when you see someone coming,

Tell him to have a good day.

Look for the answer to problems,

Don't just sit and stare.

Become part of the solution—

Your problem's no longer there!

Look through the clouds

   to the sunshine

And wink at a passing star,

Help someone who needs helping

And then you help what you are.

CYNTHIA ULRICH TOBIAS

THOUGHTFULNESS

Thoughtfulness is a beautiful character quality. A child who has learned to be sensitive to others will be welcome almost everywhere! We need to teach our children to put themselves "into the shoes" of others and walk around in them for a while.

GIVE IT A TRY

1. As a family, practice finding ways to anticipate the needs of others. For example, if the pastor is going to have a particularly busy week, why not drop by and find something on his "to do" list that you can help to accomplish? Each week, see who can come up with the most ways to make other people's lives easier.

2. Make it a point to notice even the smallest action your child takes that shows thoughtfulness. Use praise and encouragement to reinforce every act of thoughtfulness!

JUMP-STARTING
Your Child's
Faith in Prayer

So I say to you: Ask and it will be given to you; seek and you will find; knock and the door will be opened to you. For everyone who asks receives; he who seeks finds; and to him who knocks, the door will be opened.

LUKE 11:9–10, NIV

"Daddy, who's your hero?" Five-year-old Daniel was wiggling under the covers before his dad tucked him in. Dennis reached out and tousled his son's hair. Tonight's bedtime prayers had lasted for almost fifteen minutes, and it was well past Daniel's bedtime.

"I don't know, Sport. Why do you ask?" Daniel looked serious.

"My kindergarten teacher says we all have heroes and we should ask our moms and dads for ideas on who ours should be."

Dennis nodded thoughtfully and smiled.

"Well, Son, I've had lots of heroes in my day–everyone from Superman to important men in politics."

Daniel interrupted his father. "Daddy, do you know who *my* favorite hero is? *Jesus!* Jesus can do *anything*–all we have to do is pray!"

Dennis put his hand on his son's small arm. "Daniel, it's true that Jesus can do anything, and we can ask him by praying, but remember that we don't always get *everything* we pray for."

Daniel shrugged. "I know, Daddy. You're not supposed to pray for bad things or be selfish or anything. But Mrs. Hanover says we don't pray *enough*."

Dennis laughed out loud. "Daniel, Mrs. Hanover obviously doesn't know how much *you* pray! I don't know *anyone* who prays about more things than *you* do!"

Daniel looked defensive, and his dad quickly added, "Danny, I *love* the way you pray. You are a wonderful example for grown-ups. Your heart is pure and your faith is great. I am so proud of your dedication to God. I love listening to you talk to him."

Daniel snuggled into his blanket and looked at his dad. "Daddy? If heroes are people you want to someday be like, will I be like Jesus?"

"Danny, you already *are* like Jesus in so many ways. Your faith in God is an inspiration to me."

Daniel looked puzzled. Dennis leaned over and tenderly kissed his son goodnight.

"Let me put it another way, Daniel. If you really want to know who my heroes are, I can tell you right now that you are one of my favorites."

"Daddy, *I* can't be a hero!" Daniel protested.

Dennis turned out the overhead light and turned on the small night-light.

"Danny, I want to be like you when it comes to praying and staying close to God. I'm glad you're here to remind me how easy it is to talk to him!"

Dennis peeked over at Daniel, who appeared to be sleeping.

"Danny?" he whispered. "Are you asleep already?"

"No, Daddy. I'm praying again. I need to tell God what we talked about and see if it's OK for me to be a hero."

"Goodnight, Son."

⌁

God's Perspective

Someone once said
We should be as patient
* with other people*
As God is with us.
If only we could get
God's perspective—
If only we could see the world
As he sees it—
Our whole outlook
* on life would change.*

The only way
To get God's perspective
Is to stay close to Jesus,
Who gave us a firsthand view.
If only I could be as patient
And as loving as Jesus—
I know I'd be able to serve God
More faithfully.

CYNTHIA ULRICH TOBIAS

HAVING FAITH IN PRAYER

Encouraging a childlike faith in the power of prayer can literally move mountains, whether you are a child or an adult. It has never been more important to teach our children to establish and maintain an open line of communication with God.

GIVE IT A TRY

1. Make sure you are making bedtime prayers a priority in your child's daily schedule. Don't rush through the prayers–give each child time to tell God what is in his or her heart. Set a good example by praying with your children, and be as open as possible with your own needs and desires.

2. As often as possible, point out how many of the things your children comment upon during the day can be a topic of prayer in the evening. Try to get your children used to taking their praises and needs directly to God each day. Keep track of answers to prayer, and hold a periodic family celebration to offer him thanksgiving.

JUMP-STARTING
Your Child's Missionary Heart

⌒

This is the wonderful message he has given us
to tell others. We are Christ's ambassadors.
God is using us to speak to you.

2 CORINTHIANS 5:19b–20a, LB

"Dad, how do you know if God wants you to be a missionary?" Twelve-year-old Karen sat down across the kitchen table from her surprised father. Ernie hadn't expected his daughter's question, but he put down his coffee and looked at her serious face.

"Karen, God calls us in many ways," he began carefully.

She leaned forward impatiently. "But, Dad, what if God wants me to go *really* far away? I mean someplace that doesn't even have gift shops or postcards?"

Ernie looked amused. "Now, Karen, you are the type of person who will always be able to send us messages, even when you can't shop for postcards in comfort. One of your greatest gifts is your willingness to serve God *wherever* you are. You've been to summer camps, a missionary work and witness trip, and Vacation Bible Schools. You're a wonderful ambassador for Christ."

Karen looked troubled. "But, Dad, I want to know how I should be preparing for the rest of my life if God wants me to really be an honest-to-goodness missionary. I feel like I should be *doing* something."

Ernie looked at his daughter with pride. "Karen, I believe that God is very pleased with your offer to serve him in foreign fields. I'm so proud of you for being willing to leave the comforts of home in favor of representing Christ. You just keep doing the best you can from day to day, and God will let you know where he wants you to be."

Karen looked frustrated, but smiled. "Thanks, Dad. But I sure do wish God would just send me a postcard from somewhere so I would know what I'm actually supposed to do."

Ernie grinned. "Maybe God is still working on getting the gift shop up and running."

Karen was walking out of the kitchen. "That's a good one, Dad!"

↩

*G*o Therefore ...

Just when you think

You're settled,

God might say:

"Go into the desert

And look for a city ..."

And, if you obey

The voice of the Lord,

You may be sure

That God will cause

Springs of water

To appear

Wherever you step by faith,

Manna

To feed every trusting mouth—

And, from your humble candle

Of belief,

Will cause others to come

And make your lonely heart's village

A city.

CYNTHIA ULRICH TOBIAS

THE IMPORTANCE OF A
MISSIONARY HEART

It would be wonderful if every child could have the opportunity to know what it is like to serve as a foreign missionary, even if only for a few days or weeks. Even those who will never actually enter full-time mission work on a foreign field, however, can still dedicate their lives to service to God. Developing an awareness of worldwide evangelism and compassion can help your children become effective stewards of time and money as they find their places in Christ's kingdom.

GIVE IT A TRY

1. As often as possible, point out how what we do each day can affect the world in general. For example, when we give to certain charities or church campaigns, we can make our presence felt thousands of miles away.

2. Share news stories from different parts of the world with your children whenever possible, and pray for those who are in foreign lands doing God's work.

3. Talk about how God calls people to do his work full time. Encourage your children to talk to their children's or youth pastor and ask how he or she knew God had definitely issued a call to full-time ministry. When you talk and pray as a family, ask God to keep all of you open to his suggestions for what you can do to help further the cause of Christ.

JUMP-STARTING
Your Child's
Nurturing Spirit

And every tongue shall confess

that Jesus Christ is Lord,

to the glory of God the Father.

PHILIPPIANS 2:11, LB

Meagan scurried around the nursery, getting a diaper for Mommy, putting a toy in her baby brother's bed, and adjusting the mobile over the crib. She just couldn't seem to do enough to help her mother.

"Mommy, is it my turn to hold the baby?" Six-year-old Meagan held out her small arms.

Her mother smiled and wrapped the blanket tightly around her infant son, then said, "Sit down in the rocking chair and I'll let you hold him."

Meagan sat and her mother placed the infant in her arms.

"Meagan, you are such a wonderful helper when it comes to caring for your little brother. I don't know what I'd do without you!"

Meagan beamed. "I want to help Timothy grow up to be a good boy, and I want to be the best mommy in the whole world–just like you," she said. Then she quickly added, "And just like Mary–Jesus' mom." As she carefully cradled her small brother in her arms, Meagan gave him a kiss on the forehead.

"Mommy? Did Mary have someone to help her hold the baby Jesus?"

Meagan's mom put her arm around her shoulders. "Sweetheart, if she did, it would have been a little girl just like you. You are a very good example for your brother. You are careful, loving, and kind."

Meagan looked wistful. "I wish I could *really* hold the baby Jesus," she said.

Her mom knelt down beside her. "In a way, you are," she said. "When you show your brother how much you love him, you are showing Jesus how important he is to you, too. That's why you are such a help to me. You not only love your brother, but you show us all how much you love Jesus."

Meagan looked pleased. "Maybe I could just treat Timothy like *he* was Jesus," she suggested.

Her mother smiled and hugged her. "Meagan, that's something *both* of them would love!"

The Butterfly

If only we could realize

That children's hearts

Are like butterflies.

Beauty

Comes through gentleness,

Charm

Comes from fragility.

In order to be friends

With a butterfly,

You must be still

And emit the sweet fragrance

Of a beautiful flower.

Hard, cold logs

May be attractive to caterpillars,

But only the gentle flower

Draws the butterfly.

CYNTHIA ULRICH TOBIAS

A NURTURING SPIRIT

The world has never needed to be loved more than it does now. As we surround our children with love and acceptance, we can cultivate and appreciate their desire to nurture and love others. As we encourage tenderness, we can watch compassion grow in every child's heart and contribute to the survival and success of a world much in need of loving care.

GIVE IT A TRY

1. Look for ways to demonstrate a nurturing spirit to your children. Remind them frequently how much they are loved by you and by God. Point out the importance of treating others as you would treat Jesus himself.

2. Help your children think of creative ways to take care of their brothers and sisters. Praise the spirit of caring for one another, even in acts as small as feeding a pet or taking care of a stuffed animal.

JUMP-STARTING
Your Child's Stewardship

⟿

Bring all the tithes into the storehouse so that there
will be food enough in my Temple; if you do, I will
open up the windows of heaven for you and pour
out a blessing so great you won't have room enough
to take it in! Try it! Let me prove it to you!

MALACHI 3:10, LB

"Dad, I need to borrow three dollars until I get paid on Monday." Fourteen-year-old Josh was standing by the front door before the family left for church.

Roger smiled good-naturedly. "Buying hamburgers for another new kid in Sunday school?" he asked.

Josh's face brightened. "Oops–I forgot. I guess I need six dollars."

Roger frowned. "*Six?* What happened to three?"

"Dad," explained Josh patiently, "I need three dollars for the missions offering this morning. And there's a new guy–he just moved here from Texas and I want to help him fit in. Mrs. Rogers said it would really help her if she could wait until Monday to pay me for mowing her lawn."

Roger reached out and put his hand on his son's shoulder.

"Josh, that's one of the things I like best about you," he said proudly. "You prioritize your giving to God as number one. But that's not all. Giving Mrs. Rogers more time to pay what she owes you and taking the time to help a new kid get familiar with our church–that's good stewardship of both your time *and* your money."

Josh shrugged. "I never really thought about it that much. Since I was a little kid, you and Mom have taught me to give 10 percent of my money to Jesus and as much offering above that as I can. And someone needs to watch out for the kids who don't know anybody."

Roger nodded. "We've always taught you that your real treasure will be in heaven, Josh. God has been very good to us–especially giving us a son like you."

Josh looked a little embarrassed. "Aw, Dad, cut it out. I'm just a kid, that's all."

His dad grinned. "OK, Son. I'll just say one more thing before I give you the six dollars. I truly am proud of how you handle your time and money, and how you give God the first fruits of your earnings. *Your* treasure is in heaven, but your mom and I consider you to be *our* treasure right here on earth."

Josh groaned. "Dad, if you're going to get that mushy, you owe me an extra dollar!"

Roger put the money, including an extra dollar, in his son's outstretched hand.

"That's a deal, Josh. You're worth every penny!"

Faith

So many people think that faith
Is closing your eyes,
Taking a deep breath,
And plunging into
Totally unknown and
  uncharted territory.
But there is nothing that is
  unknown
Or unexplored by God—
He is thoroughly familiar
With every situation and circum-
  stance.
Therefore, when he demands faith,
He simply expects us to be willing
To forsake our familiar ways
For his unfamiliar ways.
And, after all,
Who holds the greatest possibilities?

CYNTHIA ULRICH TOBIAS

STEWARDSHIP

How to handle finances wisely is something every child needs to learn while growing up. Just as important, however, is learning to give God first place when it comes to both time and money. If you teach your children that they can't outgive God, you will give them a solid foundation of faith and a cornerstone of stability.

GIVE IT A TRY

1. Whenever possible, set the example of putting God first in your finances. Encourage your child to give tithes and offerings, pointing out that it is a privilege to give back part of what God has given us.

2. Praise your child whenever he or she shows interest in buying something for others. Even when it is not possible to actually spend the money, encourage the act of kindness and generosity.

JUMP-STARTING
Your Child's Quest for Excellence

⌐∂

The intelligent man is always open to new ideas. In fact, he looks for them.

PROVERBS 18:15, LB

"Marty, are you almost finished with your homework?" Kevin stood at the doorway of his sixteen-year-old son's bedroom, observing the towheaded adolescent bent over a huge pile of papers on his student desk.

"Not really, Dad," Marty admitted. "I just can't figure out how to do this paper that Mr. Connors wants us to write about the Civil War."

Kevin stepped over to the desk and peered over his son's shoulder.

"What do the directions say, Son?" Marty pointed to his notebook and Kevin read the brief paragraph that described what the teacher expected.

"This seems pretty straightforward. It says all you need to do is to list and describe four of the major reasons we fought the Civil War in the first place."

Marty shook his head. "But Dad, I think we ought to figure out how we can keep from having *another* war, not just talk about *this* one."

Kevin put his hand on Marty's shoulder. "Son, I really appreciate the way you give so much thought to your assignments. You know, most kids would be content to just get by with as little work as possible. But you consistently do more than is expected. That's a wonderful quality, Marty, and I'm proud of how much effort you put into your schoolwork."

Marty shrugged, but looked pleased. "Yeah, but I hardly ever turn in my assignments on time. I just can't seem to get everything done that I need to."

Kevin nodded. "You do need to try to turn them in pretty much on time. It affects your grade if you don't. I'll try to help when I can, Marty, but you need to remember that most of the time the quality of your work is more important than the speed with which you complete it. You do a wonderful job on your assignments. You go way above and beyond what was asked for. You are not content with anything less than excellence. You're doing a fine job, Son."

Marty sighed and stretched. "Thanks, Dad. Do you think you could help me figure this out?"

Kevin nodded and pulled up a chair. "Sure. How far have you gotten?"

Marty smiled and pushed a blank piece of paper toward his dad. "Well, I haven't really figured out where to start," he admitted.

Kevin groaned and punched his son playfully on the arm.

"OK, Sport, I'll get you going this time. But next time, you need to give me more warning. Let's get this thing finished and go to bed."

Marty looked at his dad patiently. "Sounds like a good idea, but it's going to be a while," he said. "I want it to be worth waiting for."

"Well, Son, let's get started!"

ig In

O you of little ambition—

Where is your challenge?

You that are content with mediocrity—

Your lot shall be a lukewarm life.

Your fate shall be an average destiny.

You must desire with all your heart

To be the best;

You must strive with all your might

to overcome the "normal" standards.

Be not content with a placid

   state of life—

Continue always

To discover,

To expose,

To reveal

The infinite riches within you.

Whenever you have decided

To settle where you are,

You may be sure that

You are sleeping

While scratching the surface.

Cynthia Ulrich Tobias

THE QUEST FOR EXCELLENCE

In a time when so many are content to put forth minimum effort, it is essential that we teach our children the importance of going above and beyond what is expected. As we teach them to strive for excellence, we underscore the value of achieving the extraordinary simply by putting forth more than the average amount of effort.

GIVE IT A TRY

1. Encourage your children to go the extra mile whenever possible. Look for opportunities where both you and they can go above and beyond what is expected.

2. Help your children identify others who have achieved excellence by putting forth extraordinary effort and showing above-average determination. Watch for news stories, read literature about classic heroes, and point out how the quest for excellence has often made a difference to the whole world.

JUMP-STARTING
a Song in Your Child's Heart

Speak to one another with psalms, hymns and spiritual songs. Sing and make music in your heart to the Lord, always giving thanks to God the Father for everything, in the name of our Lord Jesus Christ.

EPHESIANS 5:19–20, NIV

A my heard her seven-year-old daughter come in the front door after school, and knew in a moment it must have been a good day. Sherilyn was singing happily, although she was, as usual, a little off-key.

"Hi, Sweetheart!" Amy said warmly. "Did you have a good day?" Sherilyn rounded the corner, then as she faced her mom she stopped singing, and her face grew sober.

"Mom, I did *not* have a good day," she replied sadly. "No one chose me for their team at recess today, my lunch was cold and lumpy, and I left my sweater at school."

Amy looked at her daughter in surprise. "Why, Sherilyn, the way you were singing, I thought for sure things had gone better than that!"

Sherilyn shrugged. "It's a song I made up for Jesus. He's the only one who made me feel good today. I'm not sad about him."

Amy smiled and hugged Sherilyn. "Sweetheart, that's one of the things I like best about you—you always seem to have a song in your heart, even when you feel bad. Do you know that if you keep singing through the good *and* the bad times, you will make others want to join in your song and soon everyone will feel better?"

Sherilyn shook her head. "But, Mommy, they won't know the words to my songs. I just make them up as I go."

Amy nodded. "That's OK. The rest of us can at least hum a tune along with your song. I just feel better when I hear you singing, and I want to sing, too."

Sherilyn grinned. "Hey, do you want to hear my newest song?"

"Absolutely," replied her mother. Sherilyn broke into an enthusiastic melody, even though her words were a bit disconnected and did not rhyme. When she finished, her mother reached over and gave her a quick kiss on the cheek.

"Honey, that was great–I'm so proud of the way you turn so much of your life into a song. But I thought you said you were singing about Jesus. I didn't hear you mention his name at all when you were singing."

Sherilyn gave her mother a patient look.

"Mom," she explained, "*all* of my songs are about Jesus–I just don't always say his *name.*"

Now it was Amy's turn to smile. "Well, *that* explains why it's so easy to hum along with you, even when I don't know the words!"

⮌

A New Song!

I want to sing
A new song—
I'm tired of old melodies
And worn-out phrases.
I don't want traditional tunes
And conventional words.
Give me a new song—
One that's alive.
I want a song I can sing

When I don't know the tune,
And hum when I don't know the
    words.
It doesn't have to be a symphony—
It doesn't even have to be
A musical masterpiece.
I just want a song
That lives!

CYNTHIA ULRICH TOBIAS

KEEPING A SONG IN YOUR HEART

Music truly does "soothe the savage beast." Teaching our children to value music and to keep a song close to the surface of their hearts can help them stay close to the Master Musician who orchestrates our lives with such grace and understanding.

GIVE IT A TRY

1. Whenever you are together as a family, take turns letting each member choose a song to play or sing that has special meaning for them. Let each explain why the song is significant. Perhaps even dedicate it to someone.

2. Just for fun, encourage your children to put their day to music–have them sing their conversation to you, though it doesn't have to rhyme or even make much sense. If possible, record the song, and keep it in a scrapbook to listen to a few years later.